ORGANIC LEADS SECRETS

ACQUIRE CUSTOMERS FOR FREE...

ANUJ BHARADWAJ

This book is dedicated to people who want to start a new business or

have just started a business. This book will help them to generate leads

for their business which is essential for every business. I personally face

this problem during the first year of my business and I don't want that every

new Entrepreneur/business owner shall meet the same problem.

I got the solution and I like to give this solution to my future customers.

In future, If you need any kind of Loan then please feel free to contact us.

Contents

Foreword

After Covid ads cost of all social media platforms and
search engines is increasing.It is not a new thing.
In the past also they increase their ad costs to make
more profit.
Their ultimate goal is to earn more and more money
through ads. They don't think for you. They want that
you shall invest maximum money in the ads through them.
The reality is that 80 % of the money you will
invest in paid ads will give no return.
Customers you acquire through
Paid ads may not be a quality customer.
They may not purchase
high-ticket products/services from you.
They may not be interested to have a long-term
relationship
with your business.So what other options are valid to
grow your business?
Especially, if your business is small right now.
The only way is to reduce your cost per lead(CPL) to
zero.
In other words, acquire customers with organic methods.
Now imagine, If your CPL is Zero.
How many leads you may generate?
The answer is infinite.
This means you can increase your customer base by infinite
times.
you can scale your business up to infinite times.
This is how big companies became big.
There are various methods to do so.
But in this book, we learn to use youtube to generate leads.

We will learn more methods in next series of this book

Acknowledgements

I like to thank Mr Kulwant nagi and Mrs Marley Jaxx for their time, effort, cooperation

and help. Without their help, it was quite hard for me to write this book.

I have taken their consent before mentioning their name and their

content in the book to avoid any kind of inconvenience in future.

Special thanks to the team of Excellloans Pvt Ltd for their help and support.

CHAPTER ONE

Transformation

I read this from the book Atomic Habits by Mr James Clear.

There are three layers of behaviour change

1. Outcome(changing result)

2. Process(changing habits and systems)

3. Identity(changing beliefs)

There are two ways to do anything in your life

1-2-3

i.e Outcome -Process-Identity

3-2-1

Identity-Process-Outcome

Both ways are good but the problem is direction.

If you choose identity-process-outcome then

you can achieve anything in less time and effort.

Maximum people choose outcome-process-Identity

they never change processes and beliefs.

Finally, they conclude that these things do not work etc etc.

So the very first thing change your identity.

Consider yourself a YouTuber from today.

Now, what is the process?

Create content and upload content which is helpful for your audience at a fixed interval of time.

optimize your video in such a way that it shall reach your audience.

Improve your content day by day,Month on month,Year by year.

If you did it then you don't need to worry about the result.

You will automatically get the result.

If you did this 90 % of your work is done.

I will share the remaining strategy which worked for me.

When I started working on my youtube channel again

I used the same strategy and my 5th video ranked on rank 1

on three keywords. Due to this one-ranked video, my channel

started getting more views. I got my first sale just after

uploading the second video. But I am interested in the Process

and my beliefs. In less than a month my video ranked on 1st rank on

three keywords.

And if I can do it then anyone can do this by following

the same process which I am going to share in this book.

I will share everything which I did and which worked for me.

Remmember,work of player is not to win the game.

Work of Player is to play game and improve it everyday.

CHAPTER TWO

The Beginning

This is the time when I started my company excellloans Pvt Ltd.

I was facing problems to get customers.

Then I realise that this Market is very competitive.

With time I realise that not only this market is competitive but

every market is competitive. So no matter what business I do

It will be competitive.

I am an Ex banker who started my carrier in Banking on 8th of Feb 2017

as a sales office or you may say a sales executive.

It was a hard-core sales job and my job was to acquire customers

from the open market. Companies and firms were my targeted customer.

So I decided to serve the same customer base again.

During that time I learned one thing which is very helpful for me still.

"If you are not getting result then something is wrong in your process"

So I understand that something is wrong with my Process.

Once Mr Kulwant nagi suggested I create content on any Platform for

In 4-6 Months then I will start getting customers.

I was very impressed by his polite and simple behaviour.

He is the founder of Blogging cage and Affiliate booster with

an income of eight figures. Still very polite.

I approached many people but only he gave me time to

ask some of my questions. He is a full-time affiliate marketer

hence I asked about affiliate strategies which my customers

can use to grow their business.

You can watch the interview on my youtube channel for free.

Below is the link for the interview

https://youtu.be/wgFSMMWkqdE

But if you have the proper knowledge and you invested money

then only you can succeed. Otherwise, your money will be at stake.

I had no knowledge about anything except Search Engine Optimisation

but It will take a good amount of time which I cannot afford right now

because time is Money. I need customers Soon.

I was trying podcasts initially but I did not get any benefit

from podcast. Then I tried paid ads. My cost per lead was INR 600.

Now If I Acquire leads @ RS 600 then I cannot provide affordable

Product/service to customers.

Now let us think about one thing. Where is the competition?

The answer is google and Youtube.

Now why it is competitive?

Because traffic is there, Customers are there.

Now youtube and google both have Traffic.

But on youtube videos may rank within a fraction of seconds ,

if I did everything right. Hence I choose youtube first.

But I did not know how youtube works.

I learned those secrets from Ms Marley Jaxx, CEO of YoutubeLeadMachine.

For the third time, I started working on youtube.

This time I get success.

Now, What I think.

"If I am facing this problem then maybe many Enterprenure were facing

this problem. So let's share the solution with the maximum possible Entrepreneur"

I saw an opportunity in this problem.

CHAPTER THREE

Phases

For easy understanding, we will divide youtube organic marketing into

four different phases -

1. Production-This is what we do before uploading any video.

2. Distribution-This is what we do after the video goes public

3. Promotion-This is what we do so that we can get more traffic on this video

4. Data analysis-This is the most significant part in which

we will analyse data from the youtube channel.

This will help you to determine KPI for your channel.

So let's understand them one by one.

CHAPTER FOUR

Production

Topic selection

Very first thing is to select the topic on which you will create content on youtube. You know your customer better than I do. So please take time to select a topic.

Until and unless you are clear about the topic do not start production.

But I can give you a small framework which will help you to take this decision.

Market---Submarket----niche

For example, In my case

Marketing-Marketing for BFSI Products-Marketing for Payment gateway.

If you need a payment gateway for your business then below

is the link to a free payment gateway cash free

Signup for free payment gateway cash free:
https://merchant.cashfree.com/merchants/
signup?referrer=partner&refCode=CFES5172

or you can get the link in the description of my youtube video.

So I will create a channel for selling payment gateway.

I will sell a payment gateway at the front end and the remaining

products/services at the back end.

The front end shall be a small ticket Product.

You must have 3-4 Products/services at the backend

to make your business Profitable.

Of course, it will take some time. you cannot do all things together.

I recommend creating one more product/service after generating

the first one million from previous products or services.

Let us take one more example to understand well

BFSI-----Loan -----Business Loan

In this way also you can select your topic.

Keyword Research

Now, what is keyword research?

Basically, you need to know what your customers are
searching

so that you can create relevant content for your customer
which

is helpful for your customer.

I learned this from Ms Marley Jaxx.

The first method is using google keyword research.

The second is using the youtube search bar.

I am going to share both methods.

Google keyword Research

For this, you need a google ads account.

If you don't have google ads account simply create it.

The process is very simple. If you already have a google Ad account then

you can use that google ad account as well.

Simply login into your google ad account.

Click on tools and settings.

Click on the keyword planner.

Click on get search volume and forecast.

Now type your topic here.

Select a keyword idea then starts with the keyword.

Now type your selected topic in the search bar and press enter.

click on get result and see the magic of google keyword research.

Now download all keywords. You have a lot of keywords now.

But all keywords are not important to you.

Select only the relevant keywords which your customer may be searching.

Remember to select the country in which you are doing business.

Youtube Search tab

In this method, you simply type the topic in the youtube search bar then type "a".

note all keywords that the search tab is showing.

Then remove "a" and type "b" and so on.

keep doing this you will get a lot of keywords.

This is called the ABC technique.

Again all keywords are not relevant.

Select only those which your customers may be searching.

Now keyword research section is over.

Script Creation

Now you need to create a script on your keyword.

If you have enough knowledge about your topic then you
can

easily create your script. If not then watch the top five
videos on youtube.

I recommend watching the top five videos and investing
some time in knowing

more about the benefits of your product or service.

I learned during the creation of my script that your

content must have some USP which is helpful for

your customer. It must be a benefit, not a feature.

your video must have a clear agenda.

It must add some value to the life of the customer.

Try to create a hook so that people shall watch and
engage.

I learned from Ms Marley Jaxx that

you shall give a call to action during the first 20 seconds

for Subscribing to your channel and shopping small ticket size products

because people are watching videos with full attention during this time.

when you will see my video you will find that I give a call

to action with my word as well as in writing so that

there shall be no confusion.

what I say is, "if you need a free payment gateway then the link for a free payment gateway

cash-free is in the description".Even if you are selling a low-ticket product then also

you must have something free with that product. It will increase your conversion ratio.

Like free shipping in case of a physical product, free T shit with your product etc.

Read your script several times and during the recording video keep bullet points

in front of you but behind the camera at eye level.

I am a person who believes in experiments.

So, do experiments after learning and implementing the complete process.

Video creation

Initially when I started my first youtube channel video was not so good

in quality. I started to make the video better and better. But there was no one

to guide me the way I am guiding you. So I get a little improvement.

My face was ugly when I started my first youtube channel.

I focused on my face at that time. Then I was not comfortable speaking in front

of a camera. I was Shy to speak in front of the camera, especially when someone was around me.

But it was a need of the hour so I keep on my practice and still I am improving my performance.

If you are facing the same issues then don't worry. It happens with everyone.

The thing which changed my video quality was the anti-gravity movement.

I learned in an e-learning course that during speaking in any video

you need to do anti-gravity movements with your hands.

when I started using these tactics I saw that people like my

videos better now. Even today I use this tactic in each video.

I suggest you go to my channel and watch how I use anti-gravity

movement and it increased the quality of my video by many folds.

Below is the link of my

youtube video: https://www.youtube.com/channel/ UCZOoEhXP0dGA008VpauuGZQ

So, I recommend you to use it in every video and see the magic.

During video creation, you need to focus on many more things.

Background: I use a white background so I recommend starting with the same.

Do not hesitate to do experiments. But do it later not in the beginning.

Mic: I recommend using a wired mic at the beginning with a good length of wire so that you don't have to face any problems due to the shorter length

of wire.

Camera: The camera of your mobile is enough to record videos in the beginning.

No need to buy an expensive camera. If the camera quality of your phone is not good

then use the phone of any family member.

Camera Stand: Please take a camera stand on which the camera can be kept on an eye

label. otherwise, it will reduce the quality of the video.

Never ignore your body fitness, clothes, your beauty or handsomeness.

Remember, If your video is beautiful everyone like to watch it.

otherwise, customers will not make any purchases from you even if it is free.

I learned in my training in Feb 2017 that 80 % of the sales depend upon your look.

So if your video is beautiful then it will help you to grow your audience.

During video recording please take care that you don't have to make

much effort on editing. It will give you a lot of relief.

the final stage is editing. I use a cracked version of editing software to edit videos.

you can also do the same or you can get a subscription to good video editing software.

keep a gap of 3 seconds at the beginning and end of the video. It will help you during editing.

keep on improving your video. you may subscribe to my youtube channel to

know what further improvements I am doing in my youtube channel.

* Lenth of Video: Lenth of your video shall be less than 5 Minutes so that

Cold customers shall see your video. Remember people who come to your video

don't know you. They will watch your video only when the length of the video shall be small.

These days people do not have much time. So you shall deliver your content in less than 5 minutes.

Warm and hot customers will also watch your video. Of course, they can invest more than 5 minutes

of time as well but you have no control over traffic from youtube. Any kind of traffic/Prospect may visit

the video. So, I recommend creating 5 minutes of video only. Create a video of more than 5 minutes only if

and only if it is very important.

I observed in my life small things make together create a huge impact. This is also applicable to

youtube videos as well. So focus on small elements of your videos.

After editing, Remember to change the name of your video. Now, what shall be the name of the video?

It will be the topic of your video. We will understand it in the distribution section but for now please keep

this point in your mind.

* Keep your video unlisted

*do not add it to the playlist before releasing the video

*one last thing: deliver content with your heart.

Everytime I deliver content with my heart I got good ranking.

CHAPTER FIVE

Distribution

Again I learned this from Ms Jaxx.

Youtube is smarter than what we think and know.

When we upload a video on youtube, Youtube sees the video frame by frame.

So, youtube knows everything about the video.

This is why I recommend changing

the name of the video to the topic of the video.

Youtube process every data, even the name of the video.

Youtube SEO:

Remember Youtube is a Search Engine. So we need to optimise

the video so that youtube will rank your video and show the

video to the audience who will like the content.

I will give you a simple strategy to do youtube SEO.

Let us understand the terms involved in SEO.

Click through Rate (CTR): Percentage of people who click on your thumbnail after they see it.

Suppose 100 people see your thumbnail and 3 out of then

Click on your thumbnail then your CTR is 3%.

Bouns Rate: Suppose people reached your thumbnail on youtube.

They watch for just few seconds and leave your video.

This is called bouns.If 20 out of 100 people do this then it is called bouns rate of 20 %.

Remember, we did keyword research in production. You shall use that in the title, tag and description.

Now you need a tool called tube buddy. Below is my affiliate link for the tool

https://www.tubebuddy.com/anujbharadwaj83

Signup with this link for its free version. The free version is enough as of now.

This is basically a chrome extension which will help you to optimise videos.

After installing it on the google chrome extension and creating a free account

go to youtube

type the keyword in the search bar on youtube

Click on the first video

wait for a few seconds

now see on the right-hand side below the fold.

you will find tags

Simply copy them

Repeat the same with the video on the second rank

now paste tags in the description and tags section of your video

you can put tags up to 500 words only

remove tags which are irrelevant

remove tags which are less relevant

when you see in the tags section that the number of words is up to 500

save your video now.

I recommend using more than one title in every video.

Remember to copy-paste tags in the title in tags and description as well.

*Don't use a one-word title or tag. It will not rank or rank for just a few hours.

use tags with more than two words. Avoid highly competitive words like

Payment gateway, Business Loan etc.

But how to find out other titles for videos?

we will learn this in data.

How youtube will distribute videos

Youtube ranking is not only the way through which youtube will

distribute your video. There are other methods also.

1. Suggested video

2. Browse Features

3. External

4. channel pages

5. Notification

6. other youtube features

7. Playlist

8. Playlist pages

9. video cards and annotations

10. End screen

What more you can do?

give a link to your playlist in the description

give a link to your videos in the description

Set up your video in Cards so that people may see your other video.

Setup your videos in Endscreen so that people shall see your other videos

*create videos which people like to consume from beginning to end.

So, if your video is not ranking in the beginning still

youtube will distribute videos to more people

who like to see your video.

The Secret Sauce

I tried each and everything I mentioned till now when I started my second youtube channel

Anuj Bharadwaj-Excellloans Pvt Ltd. But it worked a little and I gave up due to frustration.

When I started getting leads through paid ads and my CPL was Rs 600, I started working on

youtube again and did one thing which changed my youtube career.

This is what Ms Jaxx shared but I ignored this piece of information.

What most people don't know about youtube.

"First 24 to 48 hours are most important after the video goes public. youtube will distribute videos to

more people if it gets more views in the first 24 to 48 hours "

So what I did this time. I purchase views for my video every time I upload a video.

I purchased1k views. It did not perform well.

I purchased 7k views. Again It did not perform well.

I purchased 10k views. It did not perform well.

I purchased 19k views. It ranked this time. Not on rank one but on page one.

I was thinking "how can I rank my video on rank one now ?"

I did a small change again.

This time I purchased instant views and my video ranked on rank one.

Remember, Small things make a big impact.

This was how I ranked my video.

you can implement this strategy for yourself as well.

It worked for me so It will work for you as well.

So, After uploading get instant views.

Instant means just after your video goes public your video shall get starting views.

Suppose your video gets 1200 views in the first hour.

The algorithm of youtube will be in favour of your video.

your video needs views as per the competitiveness of your niche.

I got ranked in just 21k views So I did not purchase views of more than 21k

but your video may need more or less.

So, I recommend starting from 21k views and increasing it in the next videos if required.

Keep on increasing views till your video ranks. But it will work when everything is ok.

Thumbnail

In the beginning, It was quite hard for me to create the thumbnail.

What I did. I download the canvas app on my mobile.

Then I find a different kind of thumbnail.

I select a thumbnail which I found suitable.

Then I edit its content. This thumbnail achieved very poor performance.

Then I saw the thumbnail of the channels which attack the same kind

of people which I attack and create a thumbnail akin to that.

I kept my clear picture on the thumbnail so that people shall recognise me

if youtube recommends them my video again and again via the search option, browse option,

suggested video or others.

One thing which helped me is the word"Ex- Banker".

I wrote this word in the thumbnail and CTR increased by 0.1 %

I am an Ex banker so I can write this in a thumbnail.

When I changed the colour of this word from white to yellow then CTR again increased.

Here is what I discovered from these things.

1. your thumbnail shall have your clear beautiful pic

2. you need to give the answer to your customer in just one word-why shall they see your video?

I am an Ex banker so I wrote Ex banker. Find out yours.

Remaining things of the thumbnail.

Your thumbnail shall tell clearly what your video is about in 2-5 words.

I recommend going to my channel and creating a thumbnail akin to mine

in the canvas app. Starting is the hardest thing to do. So do what I do and do

experiments when you learn how to rank your video and other things which

I disclosed.

CHAPTER SIX

Promotion

I saw many times big YouTubers went to different platforms to promote them.

I was amazed that why shall they come to this platform.

They already have traffic on their youtube channel.

When they upload their video they share them on their social media handles.

I saw it many times this thing so they are doing it.

while writing this book it came to my mind that they are

promoting so that people shall see their "Master Show" i.e their youtube videos.

So, we shall also do the same. We will use different strategies to promote our youtube channel.

1. After your videos go public, create multiple 30-second videos from the videos.

Then post them on Facebook reels, Instagram reels etc where people like to see video content.

Look for new social media

2. Lowest hanging fruits are your family and friends connected with you on social media.

Create and share your success story regularly on your social media Handle.

If there is no news then create some successful news and share it everywhere.

3. when you start earning then invest to go to big news channels etc to grow your audience.

4. when you will get traffic then collab with other influencers.

5. Think of more methods to promote your youtube channel.

CHAPTER SEVEN

Data Analysis

In today's world "data is everything".

This is true for YouTube as well.

youtube will give you some data.

tube buddy will give you some data.

Analyse those data and then decide your KPI i.e key performance indicators.

Remember I used Ex banker in the thumbnail?

CTR increased by 0.1% but how did I know?

when I changed colour from white to yellow further CTR increased.

But how do I know it? The answer is data Analysis.

One more important thing which I was ignoring was data.

Let us see the broader side of data analysis.

I uploaded a video "How to get a Payment gateway"

Now let us see the data:(Different tools and devices will show different results)

Result on youtube

It is ranked among 17 Tags

Cashfree signup page 1 Rank 2

Cashfree sign up page 1 Rank 3

Cashfree Page 1 Rank 8

cash free account kaisai banai Page 1 Rank 19

Payment gateway for India Page 1 Rank 5

Payment gateway Signup Page 1 Rank 8

payment gateway Sign up Page1 Rank 9

How to get a payment gateway page 1 Rank 20

I recommend you to go and see the video why it is ranking on

cashfree signup

cashfree sign up

cashfree

Payment gateway signup

Payment gateway sign up

Payment gateway for India

but I made video on "How to get a payment gateway "

Now search these keywords on different devices.

you will see different rankings on different devices.

This means youtube is lessening us and observing our search Intent.

Youtube knows what the user is looking for.

Ranking is low for "How to get a payment gateway"

and high for "cashfree signup and cashfree sign up"

because those customers who reach to video using keyword

cashfree signup and Cashfree sign up watched this video are more satisfied.

They may invest more time than people who reached to video with keyword

How to get a payment gateway.

In the video, I explained the signup process of Cashfree but the title was How to get a payment gateway .

you will see in every video that the ranking will change after 2-3 days as per the comfort of the customer.

If you see video today you will see something different from today.This because changes in behaviour pattern of customers.

I used

Cashfree signup

Cashfree sign up

Cashfree

cash free account kaisai banai

Payment gateway for India

Payment gateway Signup

payment gateway Sign up

in tag and description.

I feel something is wrong. It did not rank on the keyword on which I tried to rank.

It ranked accidentally on some keyword in the description and tags.

It means youtube consider on keyword present in the tag as well as the description.

After analysing the complete data of this video I understand one thing which I did wrong.

I named it Align strategy.

Align strategy

In the next video, I aligned everything according to the title of the video.

I created a video on "Payment gateway documents required".

I explained clearly what documents are required for having a payment gateway account.

This time it ranked on rank 1 on

Payment gateway document required page 1 rank 1

Payment gateway document page 1 rank 4

cashfree document required page 1 rank 1

Paytm document required page 1 rank 3

This is what youtube is doing

Just after a new is uploaded and released, Youtube gives a ranking according to keywords

which we give in the title as well as on secondary keywords present in Tags and descriptions.

Then youtube observes the performance of the video for some hours. After some hours youtube

changed the ranking of the video as per the comfort of traffic. It means when

people search "Paymentgatewaydocument required"They see my video on rank one.

Now according to the number of views, CTR, Bouns rate,

watch time etc youtube will give a ranking to videos on the keyword"payment gateway document

required".In other words, youtube gives ranking to videos according to its algorithm.

The algorithm is designed to keep people engaged on the platform for maximum time.

So, we may say content is the king but only when it reaches the Audience.

This is what we do

we upload videos and just after upload we order instant views and likes on our video.

(views are the most important factor of the youtube algorithm)

Every second 500 hours of content is being uploaded on youtube.

So competition is very high on youtube. Hence we need to match

the algorithm of youtube with our video.

Next time when you upload a new video on youtube, Please track changes in ranking and analyse data. You will understand what I am trying to say.

I analyse data from youtube and tube buddy many times a day.

It helped me a lot to rank my videos.

Keep on analysing data each and every day. It will help you to understand

how you can rank videos on youtube, how to increase their distribution etc.

Maybe someday you will help out me to understand it well.

Download YT studio app right now. It will also help you a lot.

CHAPTER EIGHT

Ultimate goal

Do you know why companies select celebrities for their ads?

This is due to their fan base.

These days Brands approach influencers. Do you know why?

Because of their fan following.

We are doing the same thing here.

The goal of your youtube channel is to create your fab base.

The more fans you have, the more revenue your business will have.

They will even purchase product/services which then donnot need.

Just because they are your fan.

Remmember to maintain good relation with your fan and followers.

In future you will observe that you get most of your customers
are people who consumed your content.

People who consumed your content will become your partners,your Affiliate etc.

So it will help you a lot to grow your business in the coming future.

Some words from Mr Kulwant Nagi which he shared on Facebook

"Most of the things in life, which make you feel accomplished, take at least five years to achieve.This can include building a profitable business, having a loving relationship, getting your book published, getting in the best shape of life, raising a kid, and every big thing which makes you feel complete.Five years is a long time. It is much slower than most of us would like. If you accept the reality of slow progress, you have every reason to take action today. If you resist the reality of slow progress, five years from now you'll simply be five years older and still looking for a shortcut."

So,Simply start from today.Stop looking for any shortcut.

CHAPTER NINE

Earning

There are various methods of earning from youtube.

So let us discuss the strategies through which you can make.

Monetisation

I am going to share a harsh reality with you that I learned when

I was learning copywriting.

"In this world everyone is selfish and no one thinks about you"

This is why I recommend not asking for help in the beginning.

When I asked for help from people to subscribe to my youtube channel.

I get a little conversion ratio. Only those people who love me

and care about me subscribed to the channel.

I shared my video on social media handles so that people may help me

by watching and subscribing to the channel. But the response was negative.

So, this time I know that people are not going to help me out

because they have no benefit in doing so.

Remember: If you need something, People will never give you that thing.

If they feel that you are growing even if they don't support you.

They will think that you are successful. Resistance of people will reduce.

Hence, I recommend in the Promotion phase share your success story.

Don't ask for help.

What shall you do then for Monetisation?

Buy 1100 Subscribers.

Upload the video at regular intervals.

Buy instant views for your video then share it with your family, friends, Social media handles etc after 48 hours when your video got views which you ordered.

Your video is ranking on youtube now, Share this news. You get 31k views, share this news.

Don't buy watch hours. You may ask why ?

Because when you buy views you will get watch time as well for free.

Suppose you buy 31k views and with every view, you get 1 minute of watch time.

So, you get 31k minutes of watch time for free.

So why not invest money in views and subscribers only and get watch time for free?

When your channel gets monetised share this news. Some people may think that you are successful.

This is why monetisation is important. You are successful in the monetisation of youtube.

"This is just the front end of your business" you know this. Everyone does not know this.

"You are not earning huge"You know this. Everyone doesn't know.

People have their own myths in their minds. Let them act as per their myths.

You are earning from every customer now. Even if they don't pay you anything.

Sponsorship:

If you want to get sponsorship then I recommend you to wait for brands to contact you.

Just mention your email in the description of every video for business queries.

If you get sponsorship but the brand does not get business/Customers then your relationship with

brands will not be good and ultimately it will tell over your business in the long run.

So, Just wait for brands to contact you. When they contact you can negotiate on your terms.

Remember the process is important not the result. You shall make yourself capable to

give business to brands not taking sponsorship somehow.

Leads

This is our primary goal. So please stick to it from day one.

Leads are the blood of any business. If you do not have leads, It will tell over your business.

Remaining all things are secondary but leads are our primary goal.

Suppose you got some leads from youtube and converted them into sales.

you will get earnings from the first sale than from the second sale, and then from the third sale.

So, the average earnings from your sale will increase. This is more lucrative than anything else.

So, from day one focus on leads, leads and leads. The remaining things are secondary.

Those customers who come to you are quality customers because they like you.

They are ready for a long-term relationship with you.

The average earnings from these customers will be high.

If you acquire customers through paid ads then they may not be a quality customers.

They may not like to maintain long-term relationships.

They may not be ready to pay you a high price for your product or service.

Hence, customers through organic means are the best customer to deal with.

CHAPTER TEN

First Fundraising

I learned this from my own experience when I was trying to start my business for the first time.

I left no stone unturned to raise funds to start my company.

But due to covid, I get multiple failures to raise funds for my business.

Neither banks helped me out nor investors helped me to start the business.

I continued to fail for months.

Finally, my mother gave me her jewellery so that I can get money by

selling jewellery and starting my business.

Later on, I saw on the YT channel of YCommbinator that every business does the same.

So, you are going to get funds for your first business from your family or friends.

It may be your father, mother, your elder brother, elder sister or your close friend.

Every business does the same. It is a proven strategy to get the first fund for every business.

Remember only those people who have money or money management skills and have love and affection for you will do so.

You are a new Entrepreneur right now
and you have no proven track record so
no other person/Organization will be ready to invest in your business because
their money will be at high risk.
So, from today focus on people who are very close to you,
and who loves your success more than their money.
Otherwise, there is no other reason to invest in you or your Business.
This amount will be very small so you will become very creative due to this reason.
So that it in a positive way.
One more thing which I will tell you that if you have no money and if you want to start a business, then this
is a golden opportunity for you because if you started a business even if you have no money for once then
you can do it again and again which leads to infinite returns.
Now you need no money to start any project or business because you will raise funds for that and every
time you will raise funds you will be smarter every time. That is why you are Entrepreneur.
Everyone does not have this capacity. Only Entrepreneurs have this capability. Ordinary people need
money for everything which is why they remain poor so far.
If you have money to start a business, then I recommend you not to use that money.
Keep that money and raise funds for your business.
Believe me, you will become smarter every time you raise funds for your business or project.

Even the founder of amazon raised a seed fund for his business from his parents.

I raised funds from my mother for business there are many more examples in this world like this.

So, raise funds for your business and be smarter not only for this time but for

every time you need to start any project or business.

When you will have a successful track record then everyone will be ready to

give you funds. Every now knows that you are good in business and their money is safe now.

Till that time only you have to struggle for funds. So, After the first success, you will have

Surplus money on your conditions.

I will guide you in future as well so that you can become more and more successful.

I will share my blueprints with you so that you can be successful in the least possible time.

CHAPTER ELEVEN

Entrepreneur success cycle

I hear about this in a weekly master class of a course for the first time, but I didn't believe the concept.

After six months of starting the first company "Excellloans Pvt Ltd," I was trying to diagnose why my

business is not growing.

During that time again I reached the same concept. This time a successful Entrepreneur and marketer.

And there is no reason to not believe him. Then I understood the problem.

My business was not working according to this system called the Entrepreneur success cycle.

So, I implemented this system in my business. Currently, it is in the implementation stage.

So now I am going to share with you this entrepreneur success cycle and recommend

you use this system in your business.

It works for all kinds of businesses so you do not need to think that it will work for your business or not.

It will work for every business.

Stage 1: Attraction

This is the first stage of every business.

In this stage, we attract customers to our business. We make our client or customer base in this stage.

The cost of the customer acquisition shall be zero. Create organic methods to acquire customers.

You are an entrepreneur be creative and think out of the box.

This will help you to scale your business faster with time you will understand its value.

Right now, just think from today onwards that how you can acquire customers by organic means.

I recommend creating one product for this stage and the give the most valuable piece to that product.

It shall be a small ticket size product.

Remember you shall not move to the next step until you earned one million at least and created a pipeline

to earn clients/customers for your business. Also, create a long-term relationship with that customer so

that you can earn more from the same customer again and again.

Let's understand this with an example.

If I want to sell this book, I will share the most valuable chapter of this book.

If I want to sell a bike, then I will create an info product related to safe riding.

If I want to sell a saree, then I will create an info product related to that which shall be very valuable for

women and recommend my saree to those women who register for that.

Step 2: Retention

In this second step, you will cross-sell to those who purchased the first product or Info Product.

Now you have not invested to acquire customers so whatever you will earn will give you excess profit to grow your business.

Remember to maintain a good relationship with your customer to sell them at this stage.

In this retention stage, you will sell a high-ticket product to the customer and Some of them will purchase,

and you will get excess earnings to grow further.

Remember that all those who will purchase the first piece of product/info product will not purchase your

first Product and all those who purchase the first product will not purchase the second product.

Only some people will purchase the next product and the next product shall be more valuable and higher in

price next time. Once again you earn one million in this stage then move to the next stage.

Step 3: Optimisation

In this stage, you will optimise everything. Everything which is not working well or not so well you will optimise that. This stage is very critical and essential you will understand this in the next step.

For this time just remember to optimise your business.

check things that are working well which are not and those which are not on basis of data.

Do not engage in guesswork.

Whatever data is saying is correct. Remember data never tell lie.

It is key guidance.

Let us take some examples 1000 people are coming on the website every month and

if the conversion ratio is below 2% to 5% then something is wrong.

If the conversion ratio of your lead is less than 31% then something is not good.

You need to diagnose the problem.

Till now my Business is in the attraction phase.

These are just examples there are many things to optimise So keep on optimising.

People who have no prior experience will tell you many things but neither lesson to them or tell them

these things because these systems and ideas are worthless to them.

They will not even try to understand these concepts because they are not Entrepreneurs.

You are Entrepreneur.

*** These first three steps are most critical for new businesses.

Step 4: Systemisation

Now let us understand why optimisation is important.

Suppose something is wrong and can you systemise something which is not working?

The answer is no, You cannot.

So, after optimisation, you will systemise the business.

This is why some businesses grow and scale and some remain small

after years because businesses systemise themself.

Now create different systems which can run the business.

Remember efficiency of a system is higher than any human as

the efficiency of the system does not reduce ever.

There are different types of systems.

System for Recruitment. System for Training

System for Customer acquisition of customers.

System for customer support etc.

Step 5: Delegation

In this stage, you appoint HOD for every department.

Now HOD of every department is responsible for that department and you are delegating them.

Let us see some examples.

HOD for HR

HOD for Marketing HOD for Sales HOD for customer service etc.

Remember there shall be only one HOD for one department.

If two people are responsible for one department then the efficiency

of that department will reduce hence only one HOD for one department.

Now give a number to every HOD. Their target will be to achieve the number.

For example, have you ever given a rating for customer service or something else?

This is the target for the customer service department to achieve a specific rating.

This is a specific number this department has to archive in terms of rating.

In the same way, you will give a specific number to every department to achieve every month.

Please remember to have a clear governance chart of your Business from the beginning.

Step 6: Automation

In this step, you will make businesses so efficient that they will run automatically. Even if you leave the business for years it will continue to run automatically.

Now you can appoint your second in command who will replace you and either you involved in those

pieces of business which are key for an exponential jump, starting a new business or taking retirement.

As a capitalist, I like to start a new business.

Have you ever heard companies hire a CEO& MD/Vice president etc.?

They may be second in command in any company.

If you don't know then no need to worry. You will understand when you reach this stage.

Step 7: Expansion

Now your business is ready to expand. The good thing is that it will grow year on year,

Month on Month continuously It will expand without much effort now.

Congratulations, on reading this complete journey.

CHAPTER TWELVE

Real Business

Business is not about the outer world. It is about your inner world.

Your self-doubts, your confusion, your confidence, your leadership skills etc.

Business and investing are team sports. You cannot do it alone.

There are three kinds of people in business

Executive, Manager(Integrator) and visionary or Entrepreneur.

Your business will not grow until you have these three kinds of people in business

You have to struggle until you transform into an entrepreneur.

It takes 3 years to complete transformation.

The First 3 stages of a business are critical.

The first three businesses are critical.

Learn to remain comfortable in an uncomfortable situation.

You will face different challenges and problems every day in the Business world.

See what successful businesses are doing and hack their strategy and tactics to succeed fast.

To succeed fast fail. Never hesitate to fail. Fail fast and learn from that failure.

Failure is the best teacher. Believe me when you think you are growing beware.

Forget whatever you learn in traditional education. That education is of no use in Business.

Traditional education is created so that we don't have to face a scarcity of Employees. Education of

An entrepreneur is different from Traditional education.

We learn from mistakes, books, coaches, consultants,

team members, attorneys, Accountants etc.

Since childhood our parents, society, teacher and everyone trained us to think that mistakes = Bad, Punishment, Pain etc. (one or all). Delete this thing from your mind.

To succeed once you must fail multiple times. Keep on trying even after multiple failures.

Someday, some week or some month you will see that your business is growing and you achieve success.

You are the asset, and you are the liability.

You are responsible for each and everything which you are facing. No one else.

If you blame someone then you will not be able to grow.

Invest in your education

Never take Paycheck or salary from your Business.

Remember, an Entrepreneur works for free.

*Most important thing which I like to share is "Business is an Art"

It works on Proved systems and Processes.

So you need to find out and understand that proven system.

Then simply implement it in your business.

CHAPTER THIRTEEN

The secret behind helping customers

I saw many people who do not want to help their customers to be successful.

They want to keep their secrets undisclosed.

They just want to earn money from their customers.

I don't know why. Here is why I like to help my customers.

I promote a payment gateway so that I can earn recurring income.

I want to earn as much as possible.

But my customers do not want a payment gateway.

They want to acquire more and more customers.

They want maximum revenue.

If I help them to acquire leads for free, they will collect more payments

through the payment gateway. Hence my earnings will increase.

Suppose I want to sell e-learning courses to my customers.

They are earning five lakh per month.

Can they buy my course for Rs 999?

The answer is yes. They can if they trust me.

But if their earnings are Zero.

Can I sell them a course worth Rs 999?

The answer is no.

Hence, I like to help my customers to earn more so that I can earn more.

If my customers grow, I can grow easily.

If my customer does not grow, my business will struggle and finally, I will be in financial trouble.

So, I like to help my customers as much as possible.

If they grow I will automatically grow.

Finally, I request you to help your customers to achieve their desire.

This is the only way for you to grow and increase earnings.

It will be helpful for you and your customers as well.

If you are an affiliate marketer then sign up 30-day free trail

of affiliate boosters and try to understand how businesses

help their customers to grow.

below is the link for the affiliate booster

https://www.affiliatebooster.com/?ref=864

Ideal Customer life cycle

There are seven stages of a customer life cycle in any Business.

Here your youtube channel is your business.

So it is applicable to your business as well

1. Know
2. Like
3. Trust
4. Try
5. Buy
6. Repeat
7.Refer

Message for Readers

I hope you enjoyed reading this book.

But your real education will start when you will start implementing

the tactics which I shared with you. I recommend reading

this book three times to take maximum benefit.

If you have any feedback or complaints then please share them with us.

Send your feedback or complaint on this email

at anuj@excellloans.in with the subject "feedback or complaints"

We welcome complaints or feedback.

Please read my other book DSA Secrets

Signup for free payment gateway cash free:

https://merchant.cashfree.com/merchants/signup?referrer=partner&refCode=CFES5172

Link for our websites: https://excellloans.in/

https://excellloans.com/

Link for affiliate booster:https://www.affiliatebooster.com/?ref=864

Recommended Hosting Hostinger:https://www.hostg.xyz/SH60V

Follow me on social media

Facebook: https://www.facebook.com/anuj.bharadwaj.775/

LinkedIn : www.linkedin.com/in/anujbharadwaj

Instagram: https://www.instagram.com/anujbharadwaj83

All links are available in the description of my youtube videos.

*I buy views from followers India

If you like to be our permanent client then, please

email us at anuj@excellloans.in with the headline #Permanent Client.

Final Word

We are looking for Joint ventures so that we can grow together.

So, If you are interested to work together then please

send us an email at anuj@excellloans.in headline shall be #JV

Alternate Email Id: excellloans@gmail.com

Stay In Touch

This is series 1 of organic leads secret.

In future, I will write series 2,3..... (and some other books as well.)

which will give you my proven step-by-step strategy

to acquire customers with organic means.

I am a full-time writer so often I write books.

Enjoy your reading.

Stay in touch through my youtube channel Anuj Bharadwaj -Excellloans Pvt Ltd

Link for my youtube channel

https://www.youtube.com/channel/ UCZOoEhXP0dGA0U8VpauuGZQ

This will help you to grow your youtube channel as well.

I hope this is the beginning of our relationship.

with Thanks

Anuj Bharadwaj

Author, Founder of Excellloans Pvt Ltd

www.ingramcontent.com/pod-product-compliance
Lightning Source LLC
Chambersburg PA
CBHW061400160726
47995CB00001B/405